THE PSYCHOLOGY
WORKBOOK FOR WRITERS

Darian Smith

TABLE OF CONTENTS

INTRODUCTION

Writing is a form of psychology. Writers – the good ones anyway – are keen observers of human nature and they capture it in their characters and storytelling. They show the behaviours, the thought processes, and the ways people make meaning out of their experiences and events and turn these into provoking entertainment.

A lot of this is done by instinct or by the gradual build-up of experience and skill. But established psychological theories and counselling ideas can help short cut this process and enable writers to create compelling, well rounded, understandable characters, and interesting stories that make sense to the reader.

My own interest in these two fields and how they might combine started at university where I completed a Bachelor degree with a double major in psychology and English literature. I followed that up with a Diploma in Counselling, became a member of the NZ Association of Counsellors and started up in private practice. I was already writing fiction in my spare time and soon realised that much of the success or failure of a story hangs on the characters it contains. A well rounded character with interesting relationships and complex conflict with other fully developed characters gives a reader something to connect to. It makes them care what happens next.

I started thinking about how to use what I know about psychology to create more believable characters to draw the reader in. I released a novel, Currents of Change, and the reader reviews started saying things like "great characterisation" "the characters are very human" and "a really fun book to read." It worked!

I've presented on this topic to writers groups on several occasions and always get a really positive response from the audience. I think because it doesn't take long to see how thinking about these elements adds depth to your characters and, consequently, your story. Realistic characters have internal monologues about themselves and the world around them, they have strengths and weaknesses, history, family dynamics, relationships, personality, conflict styles – they have psychology!

In this book, I aim to outline several counselling and psychological theories with a view to how they help writers. These theories help therapists make sense of personality, human interaction, conflict, self-sabotage and more. For your characters to be realistic, they need to contain these attributes – just like real people do.

Each chapter will outline a theory or concept as simply as possible. I'll provide examples from literature and movies to demonstrate what is being talked about and two worksheets with questions to help you apply the theory to your own work – one to help build your characters and one to help build your story.

"But I already know my characters and story!" you may say. Great. This will help you drill down into what really makes them tick and add layers to them. It will also help you bring out the elements that you know in new and interesting ways to show your readers.

Even writers with a strong understanding of human nature sometimes find it a challenge to apply that understanding to their writing. By doing this in a conscious process, you will gradually integrate it into your instinctive writing behaviour.

The difference between writers and therapists, of course, is that therapists are working to help clients resolve their issues and writers are *creating* issues for their characters! This is how they bring conflict into the story.

This book is NOT intended as a self-help book or for therapeutic use. It will condense several years of training into a few pages designed to be useful for a writer, not a therapist. The focus here will be on creating trouble, not fixing it. To summarise: This is for your CHARACTERS, not your friends and family!!

Use as much or as little as you are comfortable with. Most therapists settle on a couple of favourite approaches in the way they work and that's okay for writers too. Some theories cover the same ground but a different path so find the one that suits you best. Use what makes sense to you and throw away the rest.

But try it first. Practise and think about each of these theories and elements. I guarantee they will help add depth to your writing.

BLAME THE PARENTS

The Theory

"Tell me about your mother" said in a Sigmund Freud accent, this is the second most clichéd quote from therapists. (Beaten only by "And how does that make you feel?")

Psychology has a bit of a reputation for blaming parents for things. It's a little unfair, but there's some truth to it. Human beings learn much of their understanding of the world and how it works well before their brains are developed enough to objectively evaluate what they're learning. That means the influences of our early years have a huge impact on how we behave later in life. Parents and other authority figures, both intentionally and unintentionally, contribute hugely significant messages to our developing brains.

So while a therapist will be quick to point out that it's not actually about blame, but about identifying the root cause of an issue so the adult self can assess those early messages and beliefs with more rational logic, as a writer, it's important for us to understand the kinds of early messages our characters were given so that we understand how they operate in the "now" of the story we're telling.

So what kinds of messages are there? The counselling theory known as Transactional Analysis has handily split these into two types: Injunctions and Drivers (listed in *TA Today*, Ian Stewart, Vann Joines).

Injunctions are the "Don't" messages. On a subconscious level, they tell your character that they're not an okay person because they're not allowed to do or be these particular things. These messages are rarely given intentionally but usually picked up through behavioural cues and absorbed into the subconscious. They're a great source of insecurity for a character. They include:

- Don't feel
  E.g. Don't cry. Don't have emotions or keep them to yourself if you do.

- Don't belong
  E.g. Putting down roots is a bad idea. You're a loner and you don't belong anywhere.

- Don't be you
  E.g. Who you are isn't good enough and is wrong. You should be more sporty/academic/quiet/straight.
  You should be like your brother.

- Don't think
  E.g. Boys don't like smart girls. If I want your opinion I'll ask for it. Smarty-pants.

- Don't exist
  E.g. My life was great before I had kids. I had to give up my career to have you.

- Don't be close
  E.g. You shouldn't get attached. People hurt you or you'll hurt them.

- Don't grow up
  E.g. Children are cute, it's a pity they have to turn into teenagers.

- Don't be important
  E.g. Stop trying to get attention.

- Don't be well
  E.g. I feel good when I'm looking after you.

- Don't make it
  E.g. Nobody in this family does anything worthwhile. Don't get too big for your boots.

- Don't be a child
  E.g. You need to be the adult and look after me.

Drivers, on the other hand, are more positive messages and often given intentionally. They are the messages that drive us to achieve and tell us we are okay as long as we follow their advice. These messages can become problematic if they are absolutes. This can mean we only feel good about ourselves as long as we can fulfil the Drivers' command. They include:

- Try hard
- Hurry up
- Please others
- Be perfect
- Be strong

Internal conflict in a character can be built by selecting a combination of injunctions and drivers that function as a kind of psychological tug of war within the character as they try to meet the requirements of the messages in order to feel good about themselves. E.g. "I shouldn't be important but it's okay as long as I'm perfect." Or, "I'll only belong and have people care about me if I do what I can to please others." Or, "I shouldn't have feelings and I do, so I have to hide them and appear to be strong so as to be accepted."

Part of the character's journey is to learn about him or herself in the course of the story. Creating an internal conflict to wrestle with keeps the character interesting to the reader. They may or may not resolve the conflict. In therapy, the objective is to help a client find a way to give themselves permission to let go or mitigate these messages in healthy ways. Your character could do this through their experiences in the story – or they may not. But their struggle with the messages and their implications for their adult life and behaviour will make for an engaging read.

Example

In the Disney movie *Frozen*, Princess Elsa picks up very strong messages from her parents after an accident involving her ice magic. She receives the injunctions *Don't be you*, *Don't be close, Don't feel,* and *Don't belong*. In order to feel good about herself, she also must adhere to the driver messages of *Be perfect* and *Please others*. These messages come from the adults' fears and tell her to hide her powers and who she is, staying in control always or else she could do serious harm to her loved ones and her country. It is not until Elsa gives herself permission to let go of some of these messages that she can truly be herself, gain control of her life and her powers, and protect the ones she loves. This internal story arc for the character is a huge part of what makes the movie resonate with the audience.

Further reading

TA Today by Ian Stewart and Vann Joines, Lifespace Publishing, 1987

WORKSHEET– BUILD THE CHARACTER

Answer the questions below to use the theory in this section to develop your characters.

What messages did your character receive as a child? Below are some examples of messages – circle the ones that apply to your character.

You come first.	*I don't have time for you.*
I won't pay attention to you no matter what you do.	*It's okay to explore.*
Your needs aren't important.	*Mind your own business.*
	You're in charge.
You need help.	*Parents never make mistakes.*
If you beg and whine you can get your way.	*Don't leave me.*
I'm afraid of your anger.	*You have a big mouth.*
You're clever.	*Drop dead.*
You're so slow.	*Don't you ever learn?*
Make me look good.	*It's always your fault.*
Be happy.	*I love you.*
Keep trying.	*You're a problem child.*
You can never pay me back for all I've done.	*Work before play.*

What other childhood messages can you think of that your character received?

Which of the drivers/injunctions do these messages relate to?

How were these childhood messages delivered? What events occurred? What memories does the character have that relate?

What beliefs do they have now as a result of each message?

What behaviours do they have as a result of those messages and beliefs?

How do they adapt when those messages are challenged?

How do these messages contradict each other and what internal conflicts are set up as a result?

WORKSHEET – BUILD THE STORY

Answer the questions below to use the theory in this section to develop your plot and increase conflict.

How can the events which delivered the messages be incorporated into or impact on the current story?

What events in the story challenge the messages and subsequent beliefs?

Who are the other characters in the story who challenge those messages/beliefs and how?

How do the conflicting messages/beliefs of each character cause conflict in their relationship?

What changes need to happen in the character for the beliefs related to their childhood messages to change? What events could precipitate this?

FLIP THE SCRIPT

The Theory

Once a person (or character) has absorbed messages from their early development, it is up to them to decide how to interpret those messages and what they will mean for their own individual world view and understanding of life, people, and the way the universe works.

In Transactional Analysis, this is called life scripting. The decisions that are made about the world get locked into a storyline in a person's mind and are often very difficult to shift. People then behave according to their script – often ignoring the events of the real world that don't support the scripted beliefs.

Studies have shown that a person's expectations shape what they see and remember about the world around them. People who expect to be lucky see and remember opportunities that reinforce the belief in their luck. People who expect to be unlucky do the same.

Essentially, how we behave and react to the world is often less about what is actually happening than it is about what we *already believe*. If I think "the world is out to get me" then I perceive the checkout operator who short-changes me or the driver who stops a little too close to the pedestrian crossing as being deliberate attacks. As a result, I might react aggressively.

If, however, I believe I live a happy, charmed life, then I will react completely differently to those events and be much more likely to write them off as insignificant accidents that have little or nothing to do with me.

With this in mind, how our characters react to the events of the story will have a lot to do with their internal life script and beliefs about the world. A writer needs to have an awareness of what the character's life script and belief systems are – and find a way to communicate them to the reader without info dumping - to make the character believable. (Remember the writer's mantra: Show, don't tell.)

These life scripts often fall into similar categories or patterns. The script themes put forward in the book TA Today, by Ian Stewart and Vann Joines include:

Until – the idea that something good can't happen until something less good has happened. E.g. "I can't have dessert until I've eaten my vegetables" or, on a grander scale, "I can't be successful until I've paid my dues." Or perhaps, "I can't go travelling until after I retire."

After – the idea that any enjoyable thing experienced now will have to be paid for afterward. E.g. "I'm enjoying this walk but I'll be sore tomorrow." The person engaged in this script type has trouble being happy because no matter how enjoyable the moment is, they believe they will suffer for it afterward.

Never – the idea that the person will never get what they desire. E.g. "I'll never meet the right person for a lasting relationship." This script type prevents a person from taking the steps they need to achieve their goal because they do not believe the outcome is possible.

Always – the idea that you will always get the same result. "Why does this always happen to me?" This person sticks with a job or relationship that isn't working and complains about it without doing anything to make a change. Or they change to another job or relationship that is exactly the same as the old one and wonder why the outcome is also the same.

Almost – the idea that one's goal is never quite achieved. This person might sabotage themselves at the point of almost succeeding or they might simply change the goalposts when they arrive at their original goal, never feeling like they've truly "made it."

Open ended – the idea that they won't know what to do with themselves after a certain point in time. "I'll be great to be retired…but then what?"

Think about how you can adapt some of these internal script ideas to fit your character and his or her background. The script needs to have a logic to it – even if that logic only makes sense in the character's own mind. Often these scripts don't make sense to an adult perspective because they were set down in our subconscious as children. Part of your character's journey could be to challenge their script beliefs – thus creating internal conflict and generating an interesting personal dilemma for the character.

Other characters will have different internal scripts and different ways of seeing the world and each other. This creates external conflict within the story. Think about giving major characters conflicting life scripts to keep things interesting and have them challenge each other.

A character may have to confront the constraints of his or her life script during the course of the story. This could be a pivotal moment for the character's development and for the plot.

Narrative therapy takes a similar view on this but looks at it slightly differently. The view of the narrative therapist is that people tell themselves stories about the world, the people in it, and about themselves. There are many different stories that can be told from the same events, depending on what is focussed on. Again, how we perceive the world and behave in reaction to it is more about the story we are telling ourselves than it is about the actual events of reality.

By retelling a particular story and highlighting the evidence that supports it, I strengthen that story. For example, a person can tell themselves the story that they are always unlucky in love. They repeat this to themselves, and maybe to friends, and they point to relationship break ups or disappointments to support this particular story.

16

The same person could, if they chose, to tell a different story – one in which they had a good relationship experience. This alternative story might require more effort because it has been told less often and the evidence to support it is less familiar. However, by seeking out the evidence – that is, remembering events that support the notion that they have had good relationships – and retelling this new story to themselves and others, they strengthen it and thus begin to see themselves and the world differently.

You can see that a character who tells himself the first story may be very hesitant to commit to a relationship because he expects it to fail. The same character who focusses on the second internal story will be braver in relationships. The results in that character's life will be very different because he has behaved differently, because he believes differently, because he told himself a different story about his life and what to expect.

Again, the different stories set up an internal combat in the character, giving them a strong personal dilemma to deal with and a lesson to learn. The character needs to resolve the conflict and figure out which story to believe – or whether there is another story that suits him better.

His personal story about being unlucky in love may make him view a female character who is a potential love interest in a negative way and this could conflict with her own internal story about herself.

Another character may have an internal story or belief that money is corrupting. As a result they dislike rich people, and have bad saving habits. These resulting behaviours may be completely subconscious and the character doesn't fully understand why they feel that way.

Think about the internal stories your characters tell about themselves, about others, about how their lives will play out, and about the world.

Examples

In the fairy-tale story of Cinderella, we see a version of the *Until* script at work. Cinderella's life is a miserable one and, in theory, she could take action to change this – she could leave home, attempt to wrest control of her family holdings from her stepmother, get another job – but she doesn't. Cinderella has a life script that says things cannot improve for her until she has somehow suffered enough and is rescued. So she waits and eventually her life changes, not from something she does herself, but from the actions of her fairy godmother and the prince.

In the television series, *Game of Thrones*, adapted from George R. R. Martin's book series, *A Song of Fire and Ice*, we can see another script at work in Tyrion Lannister, particularly early in the series. Tyrion has, through a series of very strong childhood messages, developed the life script of *Never*. He believes he will never gain what he truly wants – the acceptance and love of his father. As a result, he refuses to try and spends his time (and money) on alcohol and brothels. It is when he begins to change his desire and aim to please someone more worthy than his father, that he manages to let go of this script and achieve moments of greatness.

Further reading

TA Today by Ian Stewart and Vann Joines, Lifespace Publishing, 1987

What is Narrative Therapy by Alice Morgan, Dulwich Centre Publications, 2000

WORKSHEET – BUILD THE CHARACTER

Answer the questions below to use the theory in this section to develop your characters.

What scripts does the character have?

How do they behave as a result of their internal script beliefs?

What behaviours will show change in these scripts as the story progresses?

What internal monologue stories are the strongest for this character?

Does the character have to challenge their script? How do they do this? How does the character grow as a result?

WORKSHEET – BUILD THE STORY

Answer the questions below to use the theory in this section to develop your plot and increase conflict.

How do the events of the story follow or challenge the script?

Which character has an opposite script?

How do these opposing script characters interact as a result?

What plot events challenge the primary internal monologue stories and strengthen alternative ones?

PIECES OF ME

The Theory

Another way of looking at human personality that can be useful when developing characters is Systemic Theory. This is essentially the "No man is an island" philosophy. The concept behind this approach is that we are all part of a greater bio-psycho-social system and how we behave, in some degree, connected to the people and world around us. We impact others and they impact us.

We can see how this concept works easily in the world around us. As individuals, our behaviour accumulates to create social norms. Societal behaviour impacts on the environment in terms of pollution, construction, destruction of habitats, etc. And in turn, those environmental changes impact us on a biological level via our food, climate, etc. I.e. we are all part of a global system, affected by and affecting all other parts.

A person's family, community, gender, etc are all individual systems that are a part of the whole and each impact on how that person behaves. For therapists, this means that the best chance of success in helping someone change their behaviour is to engage as many parts of the system as possible – other family members, support people, etc. I'll talk more about this in the section entitled ***There's no place like home (with the family)***.

The same interrelated system model can be applied to our internal workings. Using this point of view, a person can be seen to be a system of many interacting parts of themselves. These parts can often behave in contradictory ways, resulting in the individual experiencing confusion and behaviour they do not like in themselves.

For example, a businessman who has to make a presentation to his colleagues may have a part of himself that finds public speaking scary because of the threat of embarrassment, and another part that is good at research and is confident that he is well prepared for giving the speech. Still another part may know that the speech is important for advancing his career, and one that finds his boss intimidating. There may be a part that logically knows there's no physical risk involved in delivering a speech but another part could be fearful that the symptoms of anxiety either are or could lead to a heart attack. There could also be a sneaky part of himself who can see how he might manipulate one of his colleagues into doing it for him or fake an illness and a more moral part that wants to live a life of integrity.

How he reacts when faced with this stressful situation will depend on which of these parts manages to take over the driving seat. Some of the parts may group together to achieve what they think is the best goal.

Because each part is only a fraction of the whole person, it is unable to see the bigger picture and may engage in behaviour that advances the small goal but does more harm to the whole person as a result.

If the scared and sneaky parts get control, he may avoid the speech but do damage to his career as a result and maybe even lose his job if he is caught. If the confident and logical parts take control he will do well. The scared and anxious parts working together could produce a panic attack.

A therapist's job is to help the person acknowledge these parts and accept that they all have a positive intention but not the full capacity for making good choices that the whole person has. By choosing to access certain parts of himself while soothing the fears of other parts, he can become more in control.

For the writer, this presents an opportunity to give the character a pivotal moment in their development. The events of the plot require the character to dig deep, access and strengthen parts of themselves they had previously ignored or been unaware of, and behave in a new way to resolve the crisis. The character grows as a result and learns that he or she can be brave, strong, clever, etc.

This is also a really good way for a writer to develop a good understanding of the character's flaws – particularly for the villains. Nobody truly has the intention of being evil. A realistic villain has motives that are understandable and relatable and they feel justified in what they do. This means there are parts of the villain that may take control from time to time and have their own motivations/logic that are, in some way, for the best in terms of the villain. They may want to be loved, or to be safe, or to prevent the loss of something they care about – and the part of them that feels those things believes the way to do this is to gain power and influence and manipulation. Perhaps there is another part that thinks differently. A villain with an internal conflict is an interesting character. Remember to develop more than just your main character!

Examples

In the movie *Notting Hill*, Anna Scott is a world famous celebrity who is dating an ordinary man. Part of her loves the limelight and thrives on the attention it brings her, but part of her craves something normal as well. It is this part that needs to feel normal that truly appreciates what Hugh Grant's character, William Thacker, brings to their relationship.

While out for a meal, Anna and Will overhear the men at the next table discussing celebrities in general and Anna in particular in an unflattering and chauvinistic way. William tries to defend Anna and fails.

Anna is then caught in a dilemma. Part of her appreciates William's effort, but part of her believes it will make no long term difference. Another part of her has learned it is better to ignore such comments and this part is joined by a part of her that fears what the media will say. Part of her is hurt by it. And another part is strong and wants to put the men in their place. This part, joined by the part of her that has an excellent witty sense of humour, eventually takes over and she does speak to the men, very deftly deflating their egos. Afterward, the part that is aware of her public persona comments, "I shouldn't have done that." But we can see she is pleased she did. And, as an audience, we are pleased she did as well!

Further reading
Metaframeworks, by Douglas C. Breunlin, Richard C. Schwartz, and Betty Mac Kune-Karrer, Jossey-Bass Publishers, 2001

An Introduction to Family Therapy, by Rudi Dallos and Ros Draper, Open University Press, 2000

WORKSHEET – BUILD THE CHARACTER

Answer the questions below to use the theory in this section to develop your characters.

What internal parts does the character have?

Which are the strongest parts?

Which internal parts work together?

Which internal parts are opposites or could be used to mitigate each other?

Which parts fight each other for control?

Under what circumstances to the different parts take control?

What behaviours in the character show the reader which part is currently in control?

What is the motivation for each of the parts? (Remember, a part will have a positive intention, even if the behaviour it produces appears negative – people make sense in their own way.)

What happens when the internal parts disagree with what the character's stated goal is?

WORKSHEET – BUILD THE STORY

Answer the questions below to use the theory in this section to develop your plot and increase conflict.

When can an inappropriate part of a character take control of their actions and cause an increase in tension or extra problems?

What internal parts of one character conflict with the internal parts of other characters?

Which other character brings out a particular part? And why?

What behaviours show the reader that the parts are clashing between characters?

ALL'S FAIR IN LOVE AND WAR

The Theory

Relationships are a huge part of any story. Writers need to have an understanding of how their characters relate to each other and how to demonstrate affection, dislike, and the myriad of other human emotions towards each other. Whether it's a slow building romance or a buddy adventure, showing the reader how the characters feel about each other and how that relationship changes over the course of the story is vital to keeping the reader engaged. Plot may make the story interesting but engaging characters and their relationship to each other is what makes us care.

Literature has a lot to answer for in the theory that opposites attract in relationship. There's a good reason for this: Opposites make for good conflict! And conflict makes for a good story. So while you want two characters who will end up together to have enough in common that it seems logical that they would be happy, it can also be advantages to have them be opposites in many ways to increase the conflict between them throughout the story. Each character has strengths and weaknesses that are complimented by the other but which also clash enough to provide problems and drive the story forward. An understanding of relationship theories can help a writer bring characters together and tear them apart.

Communication

As any counsellor or relationship therapist will tell you, the key to a good relationship is communication. For a writer, however, miscommunication is just as important. What our characters say to each other is important but equally so is what they *don't say*. Letting your reader see there is more that a character is not telling sets up tension and helps keep them engaged in the story. So think about how your characters communicate, what they are willing to tell and who they are willing to tell it to. What motivates them to keep a secret and what will make them reveal it?

In relationship therapy, couples are encouraged to engage in a style of communication known as mirroring, where one speaks and the other re-phrases what they heard so as to confirm that the true message was received before they reply. In writing, of course, this would result in horribly repetitive dialogue that was boring to read. However, the essence of mirroring can still be used to demonstrate a strong empathic connection between characters. One character can observe to another what their impression is of his or her feelings/thoughts/situation. This shows that they are caring, paying attention, and have an understanding of the other character – if they get it right. If their observations are incorrect, it can spark a hearty conflict dialogue between the characters which can reveal more about each of them or about their relationship, and this moves the story along. Any of these options will be useful to the writer.

Love languages

One of the key ways to build conflict between characters who actually do care about each other is to have a mis-match in the way they show their feelings. This is often a source of difficulty in real human relationships due to a phenomenon described by Gary Chapman in his book, *The Five Love Languages*. Basically, the ways in which people communicate affection vary greatly. Chapman describes it as being like five completely different languages being spoken. Each person in the relationship is fluent in one, maybe two of the languages but they may not be the same two as their partner and this causes a lack of understanding in what is being communicated.

Chapman's five love languages are:

- Words
- Acts of Service
- Touch/Physical Affection
- Gifts
- Quality Time

Each of these ways of expressing affection has merit and there are no right or wrong ways to do it. However, if one person is communicating their love with words and expects the other person to do the same, they may miss the fact that their partner says "I love you" not in words but by bringing them breakfast in bed every morning.

The classic example might be the husband who expresses love through physical affection and gifts to a wife who expresses love through words and quality time. He works long hours so as to bring home a pay check and feel like he is providing things for her as a token of his love. He wants their sex life to be full steam when he is home as this expresses his physical love language and makes him feel loved in return. She, on the other hand, is less interested in sex because she is missing out on the quality time she actually needs to feel loved and wants him to talk to her about how he feels. She tries to get him to open up about his emotions verbally and spend more time together, which he finds frustrating because he doesn't understand the point of it. So while they are both expressing love to each other in their own ways, neither of them is able to receive the message of love because it is not in a "language" they understand.

Part of the therapist's job is to help the couple understand each other's language and begin to use the languages their partner understands.

For a writer, this mis-match of love languages is an ideal way to show problems and build conflict between characters in your story. Part of the journey for the characters is to learn to understand where each other is coming from – or not, depending on what you have in store for those characters.

The Four Horsemen
Another great way to demonstrate conflict in a

relationship between characters is by using John Gottman's Four Horsemen of the relationship apocalypse. Gottman's research identified four critical behaviours that could accurately predict the demise of a relationship. Their presence literally erodes love in a relationship and leaves the participants feeling unhappy.

Again, having a knowledge of these is useful for a writer to be able to create conflict between characters. Think about the work you have done on your characters' childhood messages, their life script expectations, and the parts of themselves that may get out of control and lead them into damaging behaviour. How could those elements be shown to bring about the behaviours known as the Four Horsemen?

The horsemen are:

> *Criticism*
> This is when you pick on the person rather than complain about a specific behaviour. E.g. "You never clean up after yourself. You must love living in a pig sty." When a complaint would be, "I find it really irritating when you leave your dirty clothes on the floor. Could you put them in the laundry?"
>
> *Contempt*
> Behaviour that indicates disgust with a person – sneering, name calling, mocking, etc.
>
> *Defensiveness*
> Refusing to accept part of the responsibility or even consider one's own flaws. Changing the

subject to the other person's flaws instead or blaming them for starting it somehow. "You're the one who…"

Stonewalling
Refusing to engage in the discussion. The silent treatment. Walking out. Shutting down the conversation.

These behaviours are markers of a relationship in trouble so, as a writer, you can utilise them to show difficulties your characters are having with each other. Contempt, in particular, is very damaging. Think about how far you want the conflict between your characters to go and how they will mend it if they can. Using the love languages can be a good way to show a reconnection. Characters will need to find ways to address the real issue while showing respect if you want them to rebuild relationship.

Example
In Jane Austen's *Pride and Prejudice*, Mr Darcy's way with love language of Words leaves something to be desired and Elizabeth has always been so very good with them. But when her family is in dire need, it is Darcy's Act of Service in coming to their aid that demonstrates his love to her. Although she does comment that her attitude to him may have begun to change when she saw his home at Pemberley, so perhaps Lizzy speaks the language of Gifts also!

Further reading

The Five Love Languages: The Secret to Love that Lasts, by Gary Chapman, Northfield Publishing, 2014

The Seven Principles for Making Marriage Work, by John Gottman and Nan Silver, Harmony, 2015

WORKSHEET – BUILD THE CHARACTER

Answer the questions below to use the theory in this section to develop your characters.

How does the character communicate? Are they open with their feelings?

Are they verbal or more demonstrative?

What body language do they use?

How do they word things when they speak? Are they abrupt, gentle, diplomatic, aggressive, etc?

What are the character's primary and secondary love languages?

How do they demonstrate these love languages? I.e. if "Acts of Service" what acts do they perform for those they care about?

Which are the character's least fluent love languages? Why? How does this match their personality?

When in a relationship that is experiencing difficulty, which of the Horsemen do they exhibit? Criticism, Contempt, Defensiveness, Stonewalling?

What do they do that shows them to be engaging in Horseman behaviour?

How does the character react when faced with Horseman behaviour?

WORKSHEET – BUILD THE STORY

Answer the questions below to use the theory in this section to develop your plot and increase conflict.

What other characters in the book does this character have a good relationship with? Why?

What other characters in the book does this character have a challenging relationship with? Why?

Which characters have a mis-match of love languages? If there are none, which characters can you change to create one?

How do the mis-matched love languages create conflict within the relationship?

What messages are missed because one character is using a love language another character doesn't use? How does this impact their relationship and create conflict in the story?

What opportunities are there in the story to have characters faced with Criticism and how do they deal with it?

What opportunities are there in the story to have characters faced with Contempt and how do they deal with it?

What opportunities are there in the story to have characters faced with Defensiveness and how do they deal with it?

What opportunities are there in the story to have characters faced with Stonewalling and how do they deal with it?

THERE'S NO PLACE LIKE HOME (WITH THE FAMILY)

The Theory

The systemic approach to family and individual therapy is based on the idea that individuals exist as part of a system and the actions of each part of the system affect the rest. It holds that the system and individual want to do their best but are sometimes held back by various external or internal forces that are part of the dynamics of the system.

For example, a young person may want to move out of their family home, but feels obligated to stay so her parents don't get lonely. The parents want her to grow into adulthood but also want to protect her so they allow her to remain with them. Everyone in this example has good intentions and the actions of each person has an impact on the others and on the family dynamic as a whole. There will be an uneasy balance of push and pull between them until the issue is resolved.

A person may be part of multiple systems that work on them in different ways. We often behave differently in the work environment versus the home environment versus when we are hanging out with friends. The dynamics of that system of people have an impact on how we are when we are with them.

One of the most powerful systems in a person's life is their family. Family knows best how to press our buttons! As a writer, it's important to think about where your character comes from and what their place is within the community systems in which they reside and, very importantly, in their family. This may include biological family as well as close friends etc. It's the character's support system.

What behaviour does the family system support and what behaviour does it actively inhibit?

Homeostasis

In general, a system resists change, preferring to keep the status quo. This is referred to as homeostasis – the notion that there is a range of behaviours that the system is comfortable with and that when an individual tries to go beyond that comfortable pattern, the system will act on them to stop it. An example of this is an obese person who loses weight and finds that friends and family members try to sabotage their diet or may even abandon them. It isn't that they want the person to fail, but they are subconsciously uncomfortable with the change in that person's role as "The Overweight One" in the group.

A writer usually needs their characters to go beyond the norm in order to engage in the unusual activities of the story. This means the other people in the system (family, townsfolk, friends, etc) are likely to exert some form of resistance and even try to punish the character in some way to get him or her to go back to the way they were. They don't like having someone rock the boat.

For a change to happen, there must be a significant motivation to get your character to overcome this resisting force and move beyond a point of no return.

Sometimes the family system is unhealthy for everyone involved but the homeostasis is so great that no one within the system is willing to make a change. In this situation there is often one person who, like the canary in the mineshaft, signals that something is wrong before anyone else is aware of it. This canary can be an excellent motivating character in a story – either as the lead character or someone the lead cares about or simply sees meet a sticky end and is the catalyst for thinking about whether things should change.

It's not just the others in the system that will work to pull a character back into their established role either. Once a pattern is familiar, people will often seek to repeat it in other systems or retreat to it when threatened. Think about how your character deals with a desire for comfort in the familiar.

Triangulation

A common element in story telling is the need for previously unfriendly characters to unite against a common enemy. This bonding technique is well known in psychology as triangulation – where two people will discuss a third person's faults as a way to feel good about themselves and connect with each other in a non-threatening (to themselves) way. "The enemy of my enemy is my friend" has a lot of truth to it in this way. If you need characters to work together, think about giving them a common goal or common enemy.

Example

In the television series, *Game of Thrones*, adapted from George R. R. Martin's book series, *A Song of Fire and Ice*, we can see the effects of a family system at play. Both the Starks and the Lannisters have characters in their family systems with clear roles to play. As the story progresses, the Starks are forced out of their roles by circumstance. The Lannisters, however, are held by force of combined will into their roles, despite their acting out in various – and at times incestuous – ways.

Lord Tywin Lannister is the tough patriarch of the family. Cersei's role is to marry advantageously and serve the family by producing the future king. Jamie is to play the family hero, and Tyrion, no matter how hard he tries, how brilliant he is, and how much he achieves, is never permitted to break free of being the family disappointment. Any time one of them attempts to achieve more than their role within the family system allows, the others in the system act to pull them back.

Further reading

Metaframeworks, by Douglas C. Breunlin, Richard C. Schwartz, and Betty Mac Kune-Karrer, Jossey-Bass Publishers, 2001

An Introduction to Family Therapy, by Rudi Dallos and Ros Draper, Open University Press, 2000

WORKSHEET – BUILD THE CHARACTER

Answer the questions below to use the theory in this section to develop your characters.

What family and social systems or groups does the character belong to?

What is the character's role within each system?

How does the character try break free or develop from their established role during the course of the story? Are they successful?

What is the role the character wants?

What is the motivation to change the role? Remember, it must be significant enough to overcome the pressure from rest of the system that wants to keep things the same.

WORKSHEET – BUILD THE STORY

Answer the questions below to use the theory in this section to develop your plot and increase conflict.

What do other characters do to stop the main character from breaking out of their normal pattern in the system?

Who is the canary character who recognises that the situation needs to change?

What are the repercussions for the canary character?

How does this impact on the other characters? Does it motivate them toward or away from change? How does this show for the reader?

STATE OF BEING

The Theory

In Transactional Analysis, one of the ways to look at a personality and behaviour is in terms of ego states. These refer to the idea that within each of us there is a Parent state, an Adult state, and a Child state. How we behave and relate to one another depends very much on which of the states we are currently operating from.

Parent

- The parent ego state can be nurturing or critical
- The internalised voice of parental figures
- Takes care of you
- Tells you off
- Is the voice that says "Look both ways when you cross the road."
- Can be bossy
- Can be encouraging

Adult
- Is logical and in the present
- Assesses the evidence
- Stays in the present
- Uses logic
- Is a good place to solve problems from

Child
- Can be free and fun loving or "adapted" in response to the rules
- Is how you were as a child
- Enjoys life – full of fun and playfulness
- Adapted child is how you were in response to rules as a child – could be a goody-goody or could be a rebel

We switch between ego states throughout the day in response to events and to the ego states of the people we interact with. If I encounter a person who is talking to me from their Parent, I am likely to respond from my Child. If they are being bossy, I might be rebellious. If they are being nurturing towards me, I might respond by enjoying being taken care of.

Think about your characters and how they will behave in each of the ego states.

Drama Triangle

Another way to think about how characters sometimes interact is with what is called the Drama Triangle. The Drama Triangle consists of three roles or positions which people tend to take up and invite others to fill the other positions.

They are:

- Victim – feels hard done by in the situation, persecuted and needs rescuing
- Persecutor – the aggressor in the situation, persecutes the Victim
- Rescuer – wants to help out and save the victim

More conflict and drama happens when characters change their position in the triangle.   The Victim may decide she didn't want to be rescued after all and yells at the Rescuer.   Thus, the Victim becomes the Persecutor, and the Rescuer becomes a Victim.

Imagine a domestic dispute in a public area.   The husband (Persecutor) aggressively yells at his wife (Victim) until a caring passer-by (Rescuer) steps in and asks if everything is all right.   The husband goes quiet and looks at his feet, suddenly playing Victim and casting the passer by as Persecutor.   His wife steps into the Rescuer role to tell the passer-by that they are fine so that her husband doesn't have to feel embarrassed.   The passer-by stays and insists on confirming that everyone is safe.   Now embarrassed and annoyed herself, the wife tells the passer-by to mind his own business.   She is now the Persecutor and the passer-by, feeling tricked and abused, leaves as a Victim.

These changes can happen in an instant and catch the participants quite unaware.   They bring with them emotional turmoil and conflict and, in the case of a story, keep the reader on their toes!

Examples

One of the storylines in the movie *Love Actually,* by Richard Curtis, involves recently widowed Daniel and his stepson, Sam. We see them switch between Parent, Adult, and Child ego states as they interact. They bond with play and movies while both in the Child ego state and Sam opens up about falling in love. Daniel, from the Parent ego state, suggests that Sam might be too young to be in love. Sam, showing a surprising maturity for his age, responds from the Adult ego state to refute this and simply point out that he is. Daniel switches to his own Adult state for the logical discussion, then back to a nurturing Parent ego state to support Sam's efforts.

In the popular movie and book, *Bridget Jones's Diary*, by Helen Fielding, there is a love triangle between Bridget, Daniel Cleaver, and Mark Darcy. They also demonstrate the Drama Triangle. Bridget is a victim of circumstance by attending a party in inappropriate fancy dress, a victim to Daniel's cheating, and what she perceives as Darcy's judgement, putting both those men in persecutor roles. Darcy falls victim to Bridget's own judgemental views and sharp tongue when she takes persecutor role for herself and also plays rescuer to her on a few occasions. The men fight over her, leaving Bridget to rescue them as well. The switching back and forth creates lots of conflict and drama and makes for an interesting story.

Further reading

TA Today by Ian Stewart and Vann Joines, Lifespace Publishing, 1987

WORKSHEET – BUILD THE CHARACTER

Answer the questions below to use the theory in this section to develop your characters.

Which ego state does the character spend the most time in?

What does this elicit in others? What ego states do other characters respond from?

What behaviour demonstrates that they are in the Parent, Adult, Child ego state?

Is the character most often Victim, Persecutor, or Rescuer?

What behaviour does the character engage in that demonstrates that they are in Victim/Persecutor/Rescuer mode?

WORKSHEET – BUILD THE STORY

Answer the questions below to use the theory in this section to develop your plot and increase conflict.

With which other characters does he or she spend the most time in the Parent ego state? Why? What would change this?

With which other characters does he or she spend the most time in the Adult ego state? Why? What would change this?

With which other characters does he or she spend the most time in the Child ego state? Why? What would change this?

What story events make the characters change their Victim/Persecutor/Rescuer positions?

How do the characters respond when the positions in the Drama Triangle change? And how does this impact the story?

CONFLICT OF INTEREST

The Theory

Conflict is a vital part of any story so it's important for a writer to understand how the characters deal with conflict, how to create more conflict between characters, and how to resolve it at the right moment.

Most people are aware of the Fight or Flight response and this comes to play significantly when faced with conflict. Sometimes the response is to face up to it, sometimes to run away. There's also the option to simply freeze and do nothing and hope it passes.

When facing up to a conflict there are three basic styles of doing so. They are:

- Submit – let the other person have their way
- Use logic – put forward a reasoned argument for your way
- Get angry – lash out and try to get the other person to submit

People use all three of these styles but generally have a pattern for which one they use first, second, and third. The conflict escalates when they move to their second or third choice. This means a person for whom anger is the last choice will be much more angry and explosive when they get to that stage than a person for whom anger is their first choice. Someone whose first option is to submit will do so over little things that aren't too important to them. The person whose third option is to submit, however, will be giving up on something quite important to them and may experience real despair when they do so.

Think about your character's style and their sequence. You can great more conflict in the story by giving characters opposing patterns.

As the story progresses, force the character to escalate through their sequence of conflict styles, thus increasing the tension and stakes in the story as the character gradually becomes more invested in the conflicts and loses more control.

Example

In Jane Austen's *Pride and Prejudice*, Elizabeth Bennet follows the pattern of submission, logic, anger. If the conflict is a small one, and in particular with a family member she cares about, Lizzie is inclined to let it go. She overlooks her mother and sisters' poor behaviour in favour of keeping the peace. When she feels more strongly about an issue, she will make a reasoned argument using logic, often successfully with her father. When pushed, however, Lizzie will turn her sharp tongue on the offender and they will feel her anger – even if the offender is Lady Catherine de Bourgh.

WORKSHEET – BUILD THE CHARACTER

Answer the questions below to use the theory in this section to develop your characters.

When faced with a conflict, does the character tend to face it, avoid it, or freeze?

Under what circumstances will this change?

When dealing with a conflict, what is the characters preferred sequence of dealing with it. I.e. which if the Logic, Submit, Anger options do they tend to use first, second or third? (Remember that the intensity increases as the character moves from 1st option to 2nd option to 3rd option.)

1.
2.
3.

What sorts of conflicts does the character use Logic for?

What are the behaviours that show this character is dealing with a conflict using Logic? (Remember that the intensity increases as the character moves from 1st option to 2nd option to 3rd option.)

What sorts of conflicts does the character use Anger for?

What are the behaviours that show this character is dealing with a conflict using Anger? (Remember that the intensity increases as the character moves from 1st option to 2nd option to 3rd option.)

What sorts of conflicts does the character use Submission for?

What are the behaviours that show this character is dealing with a conflict using Submission? (Remember that the intensity increases as the character moves from 1st option to 2nd option to 3rd option.)

WORKSHEET – BUILD THE STORY

Answer the questions below to use the theory in this section to develop your plot and increase conflict.

What other characters in the story have an opposite sequence of Anger/Submission/Logic response?

How can the difference in conflict styles between characters clash and increase the tension and conflict in the story?

What events serve to escalate each character's conflict? I.e. How do the events of the story force each character to move from their 1st option, to the 2nd, to the 3rd?

How can you use escalating styles of dealing with conflict to pace the story and build to a climax?

PERSONALITY PLUS

The Theory

The Myers Briggs Type Indicator is a well-known and very commonly used tool for identifying personality types and preferences. It helps people understand what they are comfortable doing and how to work with others who may have different ways of being in the world.

Normally, doing the test requires a series of questions which give you an idea of where you sit on four different continuums or scales. These combine to give you a particular personality type.

For a writer, the Myers Briggs Type Indicator is a great way to get a sense of your characters very quickly and to think about how to build conflict between them by matching characters who oppose each other on one or more of the scales.

There is no right or wrong position on any of the four scales. They are simply different ways of being with advantages and disadvantages for each.

The scales are:

Introvert versus Extrovert

This is the measure of how much a person (or character) is introverted or extroverted. Introverts tend to think things through before they speak and are a bit quieter to be around. Extroverts like to talk things through and arrive to a conclusion that way. Introverts recharge their batteries by having time to themselves and find social engagement can drain them. Extroverts recharge by spending time with people. Introverts may seem to have fewer friends but those friendships are on a very deep level. An extrovert may have a greater number of friends that they engage with at varying levels.

These two types may deal with a crisis in very different ways – the extrovert by talking to family and friends or going to a party to let off steam and the introvert by going for a walk down the beach to think or finding some other way to get space.

Sensing versus Intuition

The Sensing person relies on their senses and what they can see, touch, etc. The Intuitive person sees patterns in the world around them and is able to reach conclusions based on these patterns even when the physical evidence isn't there. In a high school exam, for example, a character who sits on the Sensing side of this scale will get their answers right because they have learned the facts and figures. A character who sits on the Intuition side will get the answers right because they have learned the principles involved and are able to work out the answers because of this understanding.

Thinking versus Feeling

For Star Trek fans, this is a bit like Vulcan versus Betazoid. The Thinking person values logic and the Feeling person values emotion. Each side will tend to make their decisions accordingly. For example, a Thinking person buys a house based on location, number of rooms, etc and the Feeling person because it feels like home. Feeling people go with their gut. A character on the Thinking side of the scale might make a good scientist but be poor at understanding people. A character on the Feeling side of the scale might be great with people but sometimes fail to see logical solutions.

Judging versus Perception

The names on this scale are a little confusing but probably the best way to look at it is in terms of whether the character likes to plan ahead and follow the plan or if they make things up as they go along. Someone on the Judging side of the scale plans carefully and sticks with the step by step plan but has trouble adapting if things change. Someone on the Perception side of the scale tends to leave things to the last minute and operate without a plan, making things up as they go along, but they are excellently adaptable to change.

Example

In the Disney movie *Beauty and the Beast*, Belle is seen to be a classic introvert. She likes books, spends a lot of time in her own world, and can be mistaken for a bit stuck up by those who don't know her. Gaston, by contrast, shows the worst side of an extroverted nature, loud, boastful, and desirous of attention from the crowd. Little wonder they don't get along and the mismatch of understanding of this creates some dramatic conflict.

Further reading

http://www.myersbriggs.org/my-mbti-personality-type/mbti-basics/

WORKSHEET – BUILD THE CHARACTER

Answer the questions below to use the theory in this section to develop your characters.

Where does the character sit on the Introvert/Extrovert scale?
Introvert-5—4—3—2—1—0—1—2—3—4--5-Extrovert

What behaviour demonstrates where they are on this scale?

Where does the character sit on the Sensing/Intuition scale?
Sensing-5—4—3—2—1—0—1—2—3—4--5-Intuition

What behaviour demonstrates where they are on this scale?

Where does the character sit on the Thinking/Feeling scale?
Thinking-5—4—3—2—1—0—1—2—3—4--5-Feeling

What behaviour demonstrates where they are on this scale?

Where does the character sit on the Judging/Perceiving scale?
Introvert-5—4—3—2—1—0—1—2—3—4--5-Extrovert

What behaviour demonstrates where they are on this scale?

WORKSHEET – BUILD THE STORY

Answer the questions below to use the theory in this section to develop your plot and increase conflict.

Who is their opposite on each scale?

How do they clash as a result?

What story events will challenge them in this area? E.g. If they are an introvert, can the story require public speaking? If they are strongly Thinking, how can the story require them to deal with another character's emotions?

What events play to their strengths?

GIVING GRIEF

The Theory

Grief is not just about death. It occurs any time there is a loss. When the loss is significant, like a death or a limb, the grief often becomes cyclical, returning in waves to be triggered by small things, but decreasing in intensity and frequency over time. In some cases, people can get stuck in their grief but usually processing grief takes time.

Grief is often glossed over in literature because it can be difficult to represent, depressing to read, and potentially slow the story down. It's important to realise, however, that a realistic character will grieve and a writer needs to think about how to show this. Often it's shown by having a character lashing out in anger or going on a drinking binge, but these are fairly cliché now and not the only ways people deal with grief in the real world!

There are stages of grief that a person may go through, however they do not necessarily go through them in order and they do not take the same amount of time. Sometimes only focussing on one or two are necessary to demonstrate the process in a story.

The stages may include:

- Shock/Denial – a disbelief about what has happened
- Physical Reaction – trembling, weak knees, chills
- Emotional Response – crying, wailing
- Anger
- Idealisation – seeing only the good in what was lost
- Guilt – feeling responsible for the loss
- Behavioural Issues – acting out in disruptive ways
- Realisation – understanding that what was lost was not perfect
- Learn new ways of being
- Find a new place in the world
- Acceptance – accepting the new world without what was lost

Examples

In my short story collection, *Shifting Worlds*, one of the stories shows a snapshot of a character dealing with grief over a shocking event. The story is called *Spring*. In it, the main character and his wife are dealing with an unexpected personal tragedy. The story focusses almost entirely on the first stage of grief, Shock and Denial.

While the story progresses, the character continues through the necessary actions of what is happening, outwardly trying to be strong and supportive for his wife and do what needs to be done. But the sense of shock and disbelief is shown through an unreal sense of time, strange details of the surrounding world, and metaphor that demonstrates emotion. The reader never sees the character break down, but the bewilderment and shock is clear.

Further reading

On Grief and Grieving, By Elisabeth Kubler-Ross, Scribner, Reprint edition, 2014

WORKSHEET – BUILD THE CHARACTER

Answer the questions below to use the theory in this section to develop your characters.

Which of the stages does the character experience throughout the course of the story? (Circle or tick where appropriate.)
- *Shock/Denial*
- *Physical Reaction*
- *Emotional Response*
- *Anger*
- *Idealisation*
- *Guilt*
- *Behavioural Issues*
- *Realisation*
- *Learn new ways of being*
- *Find a new place in the world*
- *Acceptance*

What behaviour do they exhibit to indicate where they are in the grief process?

How intense is the grief for them?

Does it come in waves? How often?

What triggers moments of grief for the character? Are there particular memories or items that set it off?

How does this impact their ability to deal with the requirements of their life/story actions?

How does it change their goals, views, beliefs?

How do they come to accept the loss and find a new way of understanding the world?

WORKSHEET – BUILD THE STORY

Answer the questions below to use the theory in this section to develop your plot and increase conflict.

How do other characters deal with a grieving character? With kindness/misguided good intentions/ frustration? How can this create more conflict?

What story events can occur to push the character beyond what they can currently cope with in their grief?

What happens with the grieving character has no patience to deal with this?

How do plans for action change as a result of the loss?

THERE'S A LITTLE BIT IN ALL OF US

The Theory

No discussion of psychology would be complete without some thought going into those times when psychology goes bad. Just like regular health, mental health sometimes gets out of balance.

The Minnesota Multiphasic Personality Inventory measures a variety of psychopathologies and is one way to look at where potential challenges may lay in a person's psychology. Basically, it's a chart of various traits that could, in extreme form, become a disorder.

The idea behind it is that everyone has elements of psychological disorders within their makeup – insisting on cleanliness may indicate tendencies toward Obsessive Compulsive Disorder, for example. But these tendencies are normal. They only become a disorder when they start to impact on a person's normal functioning in life.

Our characters will have these tendencies as well and it's good for writers to think about where the character's tendencies – and possible weaknesses under stress – may be.

Think about which of these elements your character has. Do they have them strongly enough to actually be a problem in their lives? Could it be a full blown disorder or is it just at the "normal" level with slight tendencies that indicate a possible predilection? How are they coping with that? Do they need help? Or is it just a tendency that is visible when under stress?

Some of the possible psychological issues that could have elements present include those listed below. It is important to note that what I describe as "mild form" is NOT a disorder and is entirely normal. It is the normal side of something that, in an extreme form, could *become* a disorder but for most people never will. This is simply an interesting exercise in character building.

- Obsessive Compulsive Disorder – in mild form might be a desire for cleanliness and slight superstitiousness. At a problematic level could be germ phobia and obsessive rituals such as checking light switches a set number of times, and having to follow prescribed patterns of behaviour for fear of something bad happening.
- Depression – in mild form might be a tendency to get down easily. At a problematic level could be incapacitating and shown by sleep disturbance, change in appetite, lack of enjoyment in pleasurable things, difficulty getting motivated, suicidal thoughts.
- Anxiety – in mild form might mean the character is a bit of a worrier. At a problematic level could mean a racing heart, sweating, trouble breathing, panic attacks, phobias.

- Bipolar – in mild form means the character may have mood swings. At a problematic level they get bouts of depression alternating with mania, bursts of energy, enthusiastic but unclear thinking, and feelings of invincibility.
- Hypochondria – in mild form, being a bit overly aware of body issues. At a problematic level, the character may have a crippling conviction that he or she has a serious illness they do not have.
- Paranoia – in mild form, the character may be a bit sensitive or safety conscious. At a problematic level they are distrustful, suspicious, and imagining threats and slights that do not exist.
- Anorexia – in mild form, a character might calorie count or exert some other form of control over what they eat. At a problematic level, they are skipping meals and not consuming enough to fuel their body as a way to feel as though they have some form of control in their life.
- Bulimia – in mild form, this could be comfort eating. At a problematic level, this is binge eating to cover deep emotional problems and then purging by vomiting or excessive exercise to counteract the effects.
- Schizophrenia – in mild form, this could perhaps be a tendency to believe in the mystical, ghosts, messages from angels or ancestors (entirely normal in many cultures), odd thinking, social isolation. At a problematic level, delusions, voices that others don't hear, and beliefs that are disconnected with reality.

This summary is intended as a starting point for giving your characters minor traits and flaws. If you're considering giving your character a full blown disorder, be sure to research it more thoroughly. There are many misunderstandings in the public awareness about mental health conditions and you'll want to portray them as accurately as possible. More information on these and other psychological issues can be found in the DSM-5, which is a manual for diagnosing and categorising psychological disorders.

Example

In the hit TV show, *Friends*, Monica is portrayed as a character who likes to be in control, cleans when she's stressed and also used to be considerably overweight in her younger years. She has transformed this obsession with food into a career as a chef, but has a tendency toward comfort eating if under extreme pressure. These traits can be viewed as being on the OCD and Bulimia spectrums, but are still within normal range. If the show were a drama rather than a comedy, these traits could develop further throughout the story to develop into actual disorders.

Further reading

DSM-5 Insanely Simplified, By Steven Buser M.D., Chiron Publications, 2015

WORKSHEET – BUILD THE CHARACTER

Answer the questions below to use the theory in this section to develop your characters.

Where does the character fall on a continuum for each of the following? I.e. do they have slight tendencies, none, moderate, or strong enough to be considered a disorder? What behaviours show this?

- *Obsessive Compulsive Disorder*

- *Depression*

- *Anxiety*

- *Phobia*

- *Bipolar Disorder*

- *Hypochondria*

- *Paranoia*

- *Anorexia*

- *Bulimia*

- *Schizophrenia*

- *Other?*

WORKSHEET – BUILD THE STORY

Answer the questions below to use the theory in this section to develop your plot and increase conflict.

How do the characters in the story react to each other's tendencies and traits?

What events in the story can pose a problem for the character's particular set of tendencies?

What characters have opposing traits? How does that impact their relationship and the story?

ME AND MY SHADOW

The Theory

Everybody has secret parts of themselves that they're ashamed of and your characters should be no different. Carl Jung described this part of a person as the shadow self and it's a vital part of your character for a writer to understand.

The character themselves may never understand or acknowledge their shadow, but the writer needs to show that it is there. These are the traits that the character doesn't like in themselves. The hints of racism, the manipulativeness, the cowardliness, and other things that it is easier not to look at, not to accept as being part of ourselves. A good writer shows their character's flaws and those flaws make the character fallible and human.

These shadow traits are likely to be the same traits that the character finds most annoying in other people. Often we find the qualities we dislike in ourselves the most objectionable in others and the easiest to decry in others. Seeing our own shadow traits in others is sometimes known as projection. We project those qualities onto someone else, along with whatever baggage and judgement goes along with it, rather than acknowledge it in ourselves. Think about what qualities your character might have, how to show them to the reader without the character realising, and what other characters they might project onto.

Example

In my novel, *Currents of Change*, Moana holds strong positions of responsibility and leadership within her community and her marae. She is a strong advocate of her indigenous people's rights and as such, in her conscious mind, is against racism. When Sara arrives in town, Moana makes a snap judgement about her based, in part, on her family name. That prejudice, which she fights hard against in other people, is part of her shadow self. Once it is pointed out to her, Moana must either come to terms with it and change her ways or find ways to prove to herself that her judgement is justified as the story progresses.

Further reading

Owning Your Own Shadow: Understanding the Dark Side of the Psyche, by Robert A. Johnson, HarperOne reprint edition, 2013

WORKSHEET – BUILD THE CHARACTER

Answer the questions below to use the theory in this section to develop your characters.

What are the qualities the character hides from themselves?

What would they find most embarrassing if people knew?

What behaviour demonstrates these qualities to the reader and to other characters without the character being aware of it?

WORKSHEET – BUILD THE STORY

Answer the questions below to use the theory in this section to develop your plot and increase conflict.

What shadow qualities in themselves does the character find irritating in others?

Who do they notice those qualities in?

How much do they project onto other characters and how much is really there?

How do they behave with the characters they are projecting onto?

How do the characters being projected onto react?

ABOUT THE AUTHOR

Darian Smith lives in Auckland, New Zealand with his wife (who also writes) and their Siamese cat (who doesn't).

He has a degree in psychology and English, a Diploma of Counselling, and is a member of the New Zealand Association of Counsellors. Darian set up a free counselling service near his home, ran a private counselling practice for several years, and currently works with people living with neuromuscular conditions such as muscular dystrophy.

He has won prizes for short stories and a novel and been a finalist for the Sir Julius Vogel Award three times.

For more information about Darian and his upcoming work, please check out his website at www.darian-smith.com.

CURRENTS OF CHANGE
by Darian Smith

A suspenseful novel about magic, secrets, a haunted house, and a touch of romance.

Haunted house. Haunted heart.
When Sara O'Neill goes on the run, she believes the tiny New Zealand town of Kowhiowhio is just the sanctuary she needs. But a dangerous presence haunts her new home, threatening Sara's chance at peace. Can she create a new life while dealing with ghosts from the old?
For local electrician, Nate Adams, parenting his young daughter alone has not been easy. Even with his help, can the house – or Sara's heart – be repaired?
Someone doesn't want an O'Neill in Kowhiowhio.
Sara's return is awakening generations of secrets.
Why has the house never had electricity?
What was the fate of Sara's ancestors?
Can she discover the ghost's story before it's too late?
The truth will set…something…free.

"Well-paced paranormal romance. . . would appeal to readers who like a good ghost story, with a little bit of history and a dash of romance in the mix."
- SQ Mag International Speculative Fiction eZine

"I really enjoyed this book - a light, but interesting read that I didn't want to put down." - The Happy Homemaker

Get your copy at Amazon.com or selected bookstores.

SHIFTING WORLDS

A collection of short stories by Darian Smith
Foreword by Jennifer Fallon

Drag queens fight zombies.
An immigrant artist hopes love conquers all.
Deep space explorers wrestle with an alien artefact.
A superhero is locked in an insane asylum.
16 stories span the worlds of fantasy, sci-fi, and literary
fiction, and cause the characters' worlds to
fundamentally change.

*"Never fails to entertain and surprise…this
collection has it all" – Jennifer Fallon*

*"Deep, relevant, and extremely readable…a superb
collection from one of New Zealand's emerging talents.
Highly recommended." – Beattie's Book Blog*

Excerpt:

There's a moment, just before waking, when I forget
it's gone. I feel the ghost of it on my shoulders, the
warmth inside. It boosts my confidence and makes me
stronger. I am more myself. I am ready to rule the
islands and mould the day to my bidding.

Opening my eyes is a disappointment. My old
bones ache with craving. It's been missing from me for
almost three decades, but I feel it just the same. I'm
simply an old man with his memories and regrets. I had
my chance. I was not worthy.

Get your copy at Amazon.com or selected bookstores.

REFERENCE LIST

An Introduction to Family Therapy, by Rudi Dallos and Ros Draper, Open University Press, 2000

DSM-5 Insanely Simplified, By Steven Buser M.D., Chiron Publications, 2015

Metaframeworks, by Douglas C. Breunlin, Richard C. Schwartz, and Betty Mac Kune-Karrer, Jossey-Bass Publishers, 2001

http://www.myersbriggs.org/my-mbti-personality-type/mbti-basics/

On Grief and Grieving, By Elisabeth Kubler-Ross, Scribner, Reprint edition, 2014

Owning Your Own Shadow: Understanding the Dark Side of the Psyche, by Robert A. Johnson, HarperOne reprint edition, 2013

TA Today by Ian Stewart and Vann Joines, Lifespace Publishing, 1987

The Five Love Languages: The Secret to Love that Lasts, by Gary Chapman, Northfield Publishing, 2014

The Seven Principles for Making Marriage Work, by John Gottman and Nan Silver, Harmony, 2015

What is Narrative Therapy by Alice Morgan, Dulwich Centre Publications, 2000

Examples

Beauty and the Beast, written by Linda Woolverton, directed by Gary Trousdale and Kirk Wise, Walt Disney Pictures, 1991

Bridget Jones's Diary, by Helen Fielding, Picador, 1996

Friends, created by David Crane and Marta Kauffman, NBC, 1994-2004

Frozen, directed by Jennifer Lee & Chris Buck, Disney, 2013

Game of Thrones / A Song of Fire and Ice, by George R. R. Martin, HBO, 2011

Love Actually, directed and written by Richard Curtis, StudioCanal, Working Title Films, DNA Films, 2003

Notting Hill, by Richard Curtis, directed by Roger Michell, Polygram Filmed Entertainment, Working Title Films, 1999

Pride and Prejudice, by Jane Austen, T. Egerton Whitehall, 1813

Made in the USA
Middletown, DE
26 August 2024

59784662R00054